Japan Diary:
A year on JET

Forthcoming titles from Eric Sparling

Treading Water (Fall/Winter, 2005-2006)
* Currently in serial publication in Angus magazine

Slawter (Fall/Winter, 2005-2006)
* Accepted for publication by an independent publisher

Fearing Fido (Winter, 2006)
* Publishing through www.lulu.com

Japan Diary:
A year on JET

By Eric Sparling

www.lulu.com

Copyright © 2005 by Eric Sparling

All rights reserved. No part of this book may be reproduced, stored in a retrieval system, or transmitted, in any form or by any means, without the prior written consent of the author.

For Tanya and Wiley

INTRODUCTION

Hey, thanks for buying my book!

The volume you're holding in your hands is not the definitive guide to living in Japan. It's not the "only book you'll ever need" to understand the Japanese. In fact, there's probably plenty in its pages to offend people who've spent far more time than I did living in Japan.

I couldn't care less. I had no pretensions of perfection when I wrote these essays. I was trying to create information entertainment. I think I succeeded.

My wife Tanya and I lived in Japan from August, 2002 until August, 2004. We were hired, through the Japanese government's JET program, to teach English in public schools. We were posted to Matsue, a small city on Honshu's sleepy Sea of Japan coast.

I was an editor at a magazine before we left Canada. At the beginning of the first year, I contacted a couple of newspapers in Nova Scotia about writing a regular column from Japan. They didn't bite and I shelved the idea. Going into our second year in Matsue, Tanya encouraged me to try again. I contacted a newspaper in Peterborough, Ontario, the city where my parents live. The good folks at the Examiner kindly agreed to let me write a bi-weekly column. Most of the columns had a prominent spot on the back page of the second section in alternating Saturday editions.

The Japan Diary column—so named by the Peterborough Examiner—ran from October until the end of July. This book reprints all but one column, although in some instances the order has been changed. (Nothing sinister about the missing column: It was a collection of short letters by Japanese students—work I don't have the right to reprint here).

Photos were an important part of each installment. Most of the photography was shot by Tanya. Some of her work is reproduced here. Rob McCormick at the Examiner attributed the full-page typically allotted to the column to her pictures. The diary wouldn't have been the same without her talent and hard work.

As for this book, my ambitions are modest. I hope you learn something new, and have a chuckle or two along the way.

Welcome to Japan.

                                      Eric Sparling
                                      Waterdown, Ontario
                                      August, 2005

ONE

Hello. My name is Eric and I am an alien.

Fear not, the Peterborough Examiner hasn't started running columns about two-headed lizard boys, lost Atlantis or people from other planets. I'm not an extra-terrestrial. I'm a foreign national living in a host country; a Canadian in Japan. As a gaijin (that's Japanese slang for "foreigner"), my wife and I were required by law to register as alien residents, and we have to carry alien registration certificates at all times (a laminated card that looks a lot like a driver's license).

In my case it seems a little unnecessary. I don't exactly blend in. With a red beard, blue eyes, and skin so pale I'm practically invisible, no one's going to mistake me for a local. Matsue, the city where we live, is a bit different in that respect from the last place we lived. Toronto has to be one of the most multicultural places in the world. Matsue is a monoculture. Ninety-nine percent of the people who live in Japan are Japanese.

It's one thing to read that statistic. It's another thing to stand in a junior high school gymnasium on your first day of work as an English teacher, stare out at a sea of kids, and realize that, to some of them, you look more alien than any person has ever looked to you in your entire life. Every day, we draw stares. Children follow my wife in the

Matsue, from the San-in Godo bank building. E. Sparling.

grocery store. Drivers don't notice that the light has turned green—too busy getting an eyeful. If there was any threat implicit in those gazes, they'd be frightening. Instead, you wind up feeling special. Noticed. Perhaps the way someone much, much better looking than me feels every day back in Canada.

If my appearance didn't instantly give me away as an outsider, my language skills, or lack thereof, would. In fairness, I'm better at Japanese than I ever was at French. That's not saying much, though. (One time, driving through Quebec, I tried to wish a gas station attendant a merry Christmas. "Bon fete!" I shouted out the window as we pulled away from the station.)

I figure I have a Japanese vocabulary of perhaps 500 words. I actually tried to add them up once. I came in at a little over 400, but I'm sure I missed a few. That, coupled with almost no grammar, means that I have no trouble asking where a toilet is and a lot of trouble speaking intelligently about international trade disputes.

Things can change, though. When I arrived in Japan a year ago, I was unquestionably an outsider, and my Japanese vocabulary was closer to 50 words than 500. When I leave Japan a year from now, I'm optimistic that I'll have reached friendly acquaintance status. Heck, we may already be there now. We've shared meals with local friends on a number of occasions. My wife and I had a Japanese couple over to our apartment for brunch last weekend—a first—and a male colleague has accepted an invitation to play Risk (the global domination board game) with some of the gaijin lads. All of the participants have to throw 500 yen into the pot, but the real victory prize is bragging rights.

What a wild ex-pat life I lead.

Time flashes past when you live abroad. The first year disappeared. I won't let that happen again. I'm going to preserve this experience in the pages of the Examiner. I'll throttle every last bit of "holy-mackerel-I-live-in-Japan" out of this coming year—and I'm taking you along with me.

TWO

Anyone who is thinking about living abroad will have a lot of questions. There's one question, though, that's almost certain to be at the front of their minds: "What's it like?" That's what this column's all about, right? Well, perhaps I can make that task easier by giving you my first impression.

Japan wasn't as different as I'd thought it would be.

The guide books always emphasize what's different about places, not what they have in common. But living in Japan isn't a daily routine of martial arts, tea ceremonies and religious festivals. One of my first nights in Japan ended with Tanya and me sitting with some friends in an Irish pub while I sipped a pint of Guinness. It was like being back home. The strain of the move overseas was eased somewhat by just how familiar, at least on the surface, everything seemed.

Most of the trappings of the West are here. We have big department stores. There are mega book marts and video rental shops. There's a McDonald's just down the street, and it even tastes the same as back home. At the height of summer's heat, a favorite stop was "31 Flavors," a.k.a. Baskin Robbins. I have yet to see someone strolling around in samurai armor, but sideways baseball caps and slumping jeans are everywhere.

Western movies are usually screened in English, with Japanese subtitles (although a matinee costs twenty bucks). The roads are very narrow, but red still means stop and a convenience store is never more than five minutes away. The cities aren't as crowded as I'd thought they'd be, either, or as expensive. Osaka's busy streets aren't that different from Toronto's busy streets, and you can get a nice hotel room for a hundred bucks.

The reason Japan seems Western initially is because it has many of the physical trappings of the West. Of course, it's not the same.

There are an endless number of differences. They're just more subtle than I had expected them to be. We have scooters in Canada and they have scooters in Japan. But in Japan, they're a favorite mode of transportation for postal workers. Lots of kids wear oversized hip-hop clothes on the weekends, but just as many choose to wear their school uniforms (in the case of girls, often accompanied by giant white socks that look like Jane Fonda leg warmers).

The truly profound differences, however, aren't cosmetic. When Canada became Canada, back in 1867, Japan had been a nation for more than a thousand years, albeit one that was sometimes divided and plunged into warfare. There's an ancient tomb under a hill less than a hundred yards from my school, and there's a shrine site an hour's drive from Matsue that's more than a millennium old.

Language is a huge obstacle to overcome when living in Japan. At first, even trivial tasks can be an ordeal. And the climate is nasty. We have brutally hot summers and, with no central heating or insulation in the homes, the winters are cold.

Finally, and most importantly, there are the people. Living culture. You could write volumes—surely thousands have—and still not cover the topic as thoroughly as it deserves.

The world is getting smaller. That's become a cliché. But it's also how I really feel. Japan isn't another planet. It's more like a fascinating part of the neighborhood. One thing's for sure: I'm gonna have a lot of fun introducing you to the people who live next door.

THREE

For a nation of bean poles, it's amazing how much time the Japanese spend thinking about food. Click on a television, flip through a few channels, and there's a very good chance that you'll come across a cooking show. The hosts will be stuffing their faces with impossibly huge mouthfuls of food, then squealing "Oishii!" This Japanese word for "delicious" can also be applied to someone who's very attractive. Even Japanese hotties can be described in culinary terms.

Cities are famous for their own distinct versions of common foods. It would be like having Hamilton renowned throughout Canada for its cheeseburgers. A Vancouverite would return from a trip to Hamilton, and the first question out of their coworker's mouth would be, "Did you have a cheeseburger?" This happened to me after a visit to Kobe. I was questioned about whether I'd eaten some Kobe takoyaki (octopus balls—tastier than it sounds). Takoyaki is a common snack—it's available everywhere—but apparently Kobe's is exceptional. Or different. Or something.

I don't know. I didn't try it.

I wasn't a big fan of Japanese food when I lived in Canada. It was always Chinese takeout in our household. The same is probably true across the nation. Demographics probably have a lot to do with this. There are far more Chinese-Canadians than there are Japanese-Canadians. Japanese food has risen in the North American consciousness, though. All those news stories linking Japanese longevity to their diet are probably responsible. Even so, if you ask a Canadian to name a Japanese food, they'll probably only come up with one or two things. Rice, of course. Then sushi. Maybe miso soup or teriyaki chicken.

It's too bad really. Here's a free idea for any of you business-minded readers: Open up an izakaya in Peterborough. An izakaya is a Japanese pub, usually distinguished on the outside by a large, red paper lantern. The atmosphere is relaxed and the beer is cheap. Most importantly, the food is fantastic. Sure, you can order raw fish and seaweed. But you can also have yakiniku (grilled beef that rivals bacon for flavor and fat content), gyooza (dumplings stuffed with garlic, cabbage and pork) or okonomiyaki (savory pancakes with noodles and sprouts, served with mayo and barbecue sauce). Top it off with a pint of Asahi draft or some Suntory whiskey, and you've got yourself a feast.

So, if the Japanese aren't just eating minnows and tofu all day, how do they stay so tiny? Well, some of them don't. The North American media have made a big deal of this phenomenon: The increase in obesity among Japanese people, particularly as Western fast food outlets have spread throughout Japan. It's happening, of course, but not as drastically as it's been portrayed. I work with three dozen adults, only a handful of whom are less than trim. Clearly, the Japanese diet is lower than the Canadian in saturated fats. There are two other

A restaurateur outside his shop. T. Sparling.

things, though, that also make a difference. One, portion size. A large milkshake here is a small back in Canada. And two, schools put a lot of emphasis on sports and exercise. Active children often become healthy adults.

I still like Chinese food, and right about now I'd murder Bambi for a DQ Blizzard. There's no question, though, that Japanese food has become a favorite. I may have to open an izakaya myself, just so I can stuff my face with okonomiyaki and squeal "Oishii!"

FOUR

I can't count the number of times it's happened. I'll be using Japanese to order food, pay for merchandise or ask for directions at a store counter. At some point in the conversation, my Japanese counterpart will tell me, in Japanese, that I speak their language well. Then he or she will follow it up by saying something completely incomprehensible. This leaves me in the unfortunate position of thanking them for their gracious compliment and then having to tell them that, for the most part, I have no idea what they're talking about.

For the record, I don't speak Japanese well. I don't even speak it passably. The first-graders in our neighborhood are little Shakespeares compared to me. I actually do enjoy Japanese, though. It's exciting for me.

I always hated French in school. I hated any subject in which I didn't have instant success. English and history came naturally to me. Math and French required studying. Forget that. My career in Canada's other official language ended in grade 11. I passed with a "D."

Our move to Japan was a chance to redeem myself. I would learn a new language—or at least some of it—and an exotic one at that. My wife and I signed up for an introductory course at the Toronto consulate in the summer prior to our departure. I'm afraid my studies got off to an inauspicious start. Even the excitement of our imminent move couldn't motivate me to study. For a few classes I kept up with the group. Then I started falling behind. It was grade 11 all over again.

That sounds like the beginning of the end. I would spend my years in Japan surrounded by incomprehensible gibberish. That would have been the case except that I made a discovery. I know how strange this will sound coming from a language teacher, but I finally realized that I do much better skipping language classes altogether. In the first couple of months in-country, I worked my way through a book, "Japanese in 10 minutes a day"—yeah, try more like an hour—by myself! Then I began memorizing vocabulary out of the dictionary. Finally, I got a kana workbook—kana is the Japanese "alphabet"—and made a point of using my free time before first period at school to work on that.

All of these steps, combined with a shameless willingness to sound like an uneducated twit, have combined to provide me with what I generously refer to as "survival" Japanese. Forget grammar. Vocabulary, baby, all the way. If your vocabulary's large enough, and you've got plenty of time, you can say just about anything that really matters, albeit crudely. This method works particularly well in Japan where, as a rule, everyone goes out of their way to be generous and kind to strangers, particularly foreign ones.

Let's use an example. Say I want to send a package at the post office, but I have a tricky request, like sending it registered and overnight. Now, if I'm smart, I will have already asked one of my coworkers how to do this. But let's say I'm not smart. No problem. I'll make my request in broken Japanese—wrong particles, incorrect tenses, strange word choices—and then I wait to see what happens. Sometimes they say something back. I might understand a third of it. No problem. I just keep repeating what I want until one of two things happens: they take the package from me, hopefully to be delivered (upon receipt of a signature) the next day; or they don't, in which case I abandon my plan.

Granted, the "Eric Method of Language Acquisition and Usage" will frequently try your patience, and the outcome from any request is always a big question mark. But, if you're like me and always considered yourself hopeless at foreign languages, I would urge you to reconsider: Don't give up—you too can speak a foreign language like a three-year old!

FIVE

I have been remiss in my duties as a tour guide. It's all well and fine to talk about food and fashion, gaijin and guidebooks, but a complete mental picture of the places and experiences I'm going to write about requires more than that. Just as a scene in a movie needs an establishing shot to orient the viewer, so does any discussion about an entire country. So, if you will indulge me just a little, I'd like to take this time we have together to tell you a little bit of general information about Japan—the land and the nation.

For starters, it's not Japan. It's not usually even Nippon. Locals call it Nihon (pronounced "knee-hone"). The Japanese refer to themselves as Nihonjin—"jin," in this case, meaning people. The Nihonjin speak Nihongo. While "go" is also Japanese for "five," here it means language.

Nihon is an island nation. There are four large islands, plus a huge number of smaller islands (the best known of which is Okinawa). Honshu is the biggest of Japan's four main islands. The other three, in descending order by size, are Hokkaido to the north, Kyushu to the south-west, and Shikoku to the south. Most of the cities you've heard of—Tokyo, Osaka, Kyoto, Hiroshima—are located on Honshu. So is Matsue, the city where my wife and I live. We're a few hours drive north of Hiroshima and six hours north-west of Osaka.

When you try to picture a Japanese landscape, one thing probably comes to mind: A packed metropolis—narrow streets, garish neon signs, and people, people, people. It's not an entirely inaccurate image. The greater Tokyo area, depending upon how you define it, has a population not much smaller than Canada's. That's right: One urban area with well over 20 million people.

If you take a look at some statistics on www.worldatlas.com, you'll find further confirmation of this picture. Japan has a population of 128,000,000 people and a land area of 376,520 square kilometers. For comparison, Canada has a population of 31,902,268 and a land area of 9,220,970 square kilometers. What the heck does all that mean?

Well, it means that Japan has more than four times the population of Canada. Stretch those math muscles a little further and you'll also see that Japan's land area would fit into Canada more than 24 times. The population density of Japan is roughly one hundred times that of Canada.

Crowded indeed.

It's hard to argue with numbers, but numbers don't tell the whole story. For example, while Japan has roughly double the population of the United Kingdom, it also has 50-percent more land. And as anyone who has ever been to the U.K. can testify, get out of the cities and you'll find some of the most beautiful countryside in the world. The same applies to Japan.

Once you leave the main population centers—most of which run down the eastern and southern sides of Honshu—life in Japan takes on a

Tottori dunes. T. Sparling.

distinctly country flavor.

Take Shimane-ken, for example. That's the prefecture in which Matsue, our city, is located. Shimane is tied with its neighboring "ken", Tottori, for being the "most rural" prefecture (I've been told that the title shifts back and forth). Matsue is the capital—it's the largest city in Shimane—but it's still relatively small. There are a few more cities, none of which are significantly larger than Peterborough. The rest of the prefecture consists of small towns, fishing villages, large tracts of mountain and forest, and a coastline that reminds me a little of Northern California. Neighboring Tottori is much the same—two mid-sized cities, with tree-topped mountains in the interior and miles of beaches along the coast.

It would be disingenuous to claim that Japan isn't a highly-urbanized nation. It is. But just off the well-worn track of tourist highlights, there is another Japan; one that, yes, has its share of neon lights and cramped streets, but also has rice paddies and farmhouses, mountain shrines and winding, coastal roads. Nihon is no more one vast city than Canada is one giant snowdrift.

SIX

It's December and I can still walk around in a sweatshirt. I was chatting with my folks on the phone the other day. I asked about the weather in Peterborough. "Minus-five and dropping," was the response.

Minus-five. We'll only see that temperature in Matsue a handful of times this winter.

Before you completely hate me, though, there are some mitigating factors to keep in mind. The big one is this: Japanese homes and schools aren't insulated and they don't have central heating. When I get out of bed in the morning in February, the temperature inside and outside our apartment will be virtually the same. Last winter, the floor in the staff bathroom at Tanya's school had ice on it.

There's something weird going on over here. I mean, surely the concept of insulation has made it across the ocean? How about sealed windows? Oh, I'm sure a few homes have them, but they aren't the norm. I'll never forget a conversation I had at the hospital with a pharmacist who had lived in the States. We were talking about this very subject. She said, "Sometimes it seems kind of primitive," or words to that effect.

I was relieved that it isn't just the foreigners who find it bizarre.

Matsue castle in a snowstorm. T. Sparling.

You have to throw on a jacket at school when you go to teach a class. In older schools, the only heat in a classroom comes from a single kerosene space heater. The kerosene heaters are a real piece of work. The one in our lunch room smells of gas. We have a newer model at our apartment. We've never used it. The thing terrifies me. We also have an electric heater. It costs a fortune to run and the warm breeze it emits is a poor champion against unsealed windows and uninsulated walls.

The madness doesn't stop at skating rinks in school washrooms. It extends to clothing as well. Japanese students wear uniforms to school. The girls' uniform consists of a blazer and a plaid skirt. Wearing your skirt extremely short is very hip. Wearing tights isn't. Then there was the elementary school student I saw walking to school one day last winter, dressed only in a shirt and shorts. He was using an umbrella to break the impact of the driving snow. In Canada, the parents would have had a visit from social services. I doubt that happened here.

It's not all madness. There is one device that saved us from turning into meatsicles last winter. It's called a kotatsu. It's a low table with quilts draping down on all four sides and a quilt underneath it. Best of all, the underside of the table contains a heater. Set that bad boy up in front of the television and you're ready to comfortably hibernate through the worst winds from Siberia. Of course, the whole thing would be redundant if the Japanese just built their homes with materials and technology that were old when I was young.

So, why do so many people here insist upon leaving themselves at the whim of the elements? Well, I don't know for sure. I think it might be part of the same mind-set that sees elementary students during summer vacation exercising in the school yard at the crack of dawn. Or the ethic which insists that the students clean the floors of the school with a worn rag instead of a mop. In short, many of the Japanese, like boot camp sergeants, see virtue in hardship for its own sake.

Just call him Colonel Santa. In what must be one of the more bizarre transplants of American culture to Japan, it is a tradition in Matsue to have KFC on Christmas Eve. But if you want Kentucky's most famous export on December 24th, you better order early. Tanya and I tried to get some last holiday season. There was a lineup of customers waiting to pick up their pre-ordered buckets. When I went up to the counter, I was told that the wait for fried chicken would be hours (although the less popular, broiled variety was available immediately). Just a thought: Maybe Tim Horton's should open a franchise over here. They could start a new, Canadian tradition. Call it the Christmas Day Dozen.

SEVEN

To call the Japanese gracious hosts would be an understatement. The kindnesses lavished on guests in this country border on embarrassing.

Two Christmases in a row I have been invited to visit a kindergarten to play Santa Claus. It's not exactly onerous work. The kids are adorable, as kindergartners are everywhere. ("Yeah, especially in small doses," mutters the reader with young children.) The teachers speak little English, but they're very forgiving of my atrocious Japanese.

On both occasions, after my mission was completed—perhaps an hour's work, in total—the tables were turned and the erstwhile Santa became the recipient of gifts. This year, the school sent me off with a gift bag containing a box of individually-wrapped cookies, five slices of cake and, the booty of all booty, beer coupons to the tune of 4,000 yen. It was almost the same thing last year.

It's not like I was doing them a favor. It's my job. My work hours are from eight-fifteen to four each day. I was being paid by my school board to be there.

Big deal, you say: A few cookies, a slice or five of cake, and enough beer to fuel a weekend-long bender for two.

"Sure, Eric, it's generous, but not 'embarrassingly' generous."

No problem. That was just a warm up. The truly gratuitous kindnesses don't take place at work. No, the shamelessly nice gestures are saved for house guests.

Tanya and I have been the recipients of this kind of generosity on numerous occasions. There was the meal we had at the condo of a young professional couple. She's a teacher, he's a doctor. After a sumptuous dinner, just before leaving, the husband asked me which I preferred, scotch or bourbon. I said bourbon. He went to a closet and produced a bottle of Booker's, which sells for about seventy bucks in Canada. He gave us the bottle to take home.

On another occasion, one of my coworkers invited Tanya and I for dinner with his family. This teacher loves to travel. He and I have discussed our dream destinations on numerous occasions. One of mine is Antarctica. Well, when the meal finished, we were served whiskey. The teacher then revealed to us that the ice chunks in the drinks were from Antarctica. The Japanese army (the Self Defense Force, or SDF) had supplied him with a block of ice from the seventh continent to use in his science classes at school. Having invited us for dinner and, knowing my interest in Antarctica, he'd brought a fist-sized chunk home for our beverages.

Then there was the time the mother of one of Tanya's students wanted to thank my wife for helping her daughter prepare for an English contest. We were invited over to the family residence for, again, dinner. After we ate, the mother insisted upon Tanya and me donning yukata (summer-weight robes, like kimono) to wear while she
performed the tea ceremony, a treat in itself. When the evening came to a close, the mother insisted

upon Tanya keeping the yukata she'd borrowed for the ceremony. The daughter still shows up at our door from time to time with food.

Most recently, Tanya and I were invited to a Saturday morning mochi-making party. Mochi is a dumpling made from pounded rice and filled with sweet, red bean jam. It's a traditional treat for New Year's. The party ended up being a large affair, with three families—plus us—in attendance. After the mochi were made, we all sat down to a huge lunch. Everything was made from scratch. Even the rice was grown by a neighbor. We were sent home, stuffed to the gills, with a dozen mochi in a box.

There's really only one drawback to all this goodwill: You want to return the favor.

Tanya and I try our best. When we go away on trips, we bring back "omiyage" (a souvenir gift that's given to colleagues—usually edible). The real test, though, is on the home turf.

We're having a party tomorrow night. It's our turn to play host. Yesterday, we implemented a scorched earth policy on clutter in our apartment. Today, we shopped and Tanya cooked. Tomorrow, we will attempt the impossible: Impress the locals at their own game.

EIGHT

The second half of the twentieth century has provided us with many examples of nations fractured by internal strife or external factors. The three examples that come most readily to my mind, though, are Germany, Vietnam and Korea. All three were split in two. Germany and Vietnam are now unified, the former a victory for capitalism and democracy and the latter a victory for communism. Korea's rift, however, remains.

I'm not going to pretend to know much about Korea. I have only the vaguest sense of the details of the Korean War. I have only cursory knowledge of the nuclear arms crisis in North Korea. What took Tanya and me to Korea this past week was something far less profound than geopolitics or Cold War culture. We went because it was the cheapest place we could fly to from our local airport.

Last Christmas holiday, Tanya and I went to New Zealand for two weeks. This Christmas we wanted to spend less money. Much less. When Tanya came home from work with a flyer advertising a three night trip to Seoul—hotel and air for around $350 each—I knew we'd found our winter vacation.

Barbed wire at the DMZ. T. Sparling.

It was a chance to get away, a chance to visit mainland Asia and an opportunity to go to the DMZ (De-Militarized Zone), the no-man's land that separates North and South Korea. Countries run by Stalinist regimes are a dying breed. I thought I should take the opportunity to stare at one through a fence.

What I didn't expect was to like Korea so much.

Seoul defied stereotyping. Yes, Korea is a divided nation, but many of its divisions are more subtle and interesting than the one at the heavily fortified border.

Our first night we ended up in a chic little drinking spot high above the street, with walls of glass and an ambiance that dripped cosmopolitan cool. It wasn't long before our server struck up a conversation.

It turned out that the young woman was the owner. Min-Kyung Park proceeded to spend half an hour helping us map out a sightseeing route for the following day. Biographical details were also forthcoming. She is a magazine photographer as well as an entrepreneur. She did her masters in fine art in London. And she'd never been to the DMZ.

Sure, it was just one person, but in our short conversation, something became very clear. This wasn't a person—or a place for that matter—defined solely by a national tragedy. Ms. Park was urbane and globally sophisticated. She was a member of that class you occasionally encounter when you live abroad: A citizen of the world.

The city itself had an energy which, while difficult to define, seems somehow to be missing from most of the big Japanese cities I've visited.

Seoul Tower rises over the downtown. T. Sparling.

Don't get me wrong. I like Osaka. It's nice. But that's the problem. "Nice" is such a bland word.

Seoul isn't nice, it's exciting. Where Osaka is a phalanx of pedestrians and vehicles, Seoul is a mosh pit.

Scooters weave their way through sidewalks crowded with Seouls (What else should I call residents of the city?). I met service people who slipped from Korean to Japanese and then into English. On one corner, we found a Body Shop and Starbucks; on another, a vendor with a steaming pot of what looked a heck of a lot like insect porridge. Some city blocks—the ones around our hotel, actually—were squalid, while others were sparkling with fantastic displays of Christmas lights.

Ancient and modern, eastern and western, dingy and gleaming, claustrophobic and monumental, friendly and indifferent—vibrant contrasts were everywhere. There may have been some grime but the pace left no room for cobwebs.

And what of the DMZ, the corridor of land mines and barbed wire that keeps a nation apart? Well, it was pretty good. The view was obscured by fog. We got some great souvenirs, though, including a DMZ piggy bank and commemorative barbed wire!

One amusing highlight: The film at a South Korean visitor's center. In this propagandized version of reality, the DMZ was an ecological godsend, a haven for flora and fauna, untainted by humans for half a century. To paraphrase: "If flowers, birds and animals can live in peace, then so can we."

A clearly bad conflict was spun into something supposedly good, a kindergarten message of Nature's disparate kingdom coming together in harmony.

But what is political fiction at the DMZ is reality an hour south in Seoul. Diversity is the city's lifeblood.

NINE

I've told you about Japanese hospitality and Kentucky-fried Christmas. But I have failed to tell you much about the place where I spend thirty-five hours every week: School.

That's why I'm in Japan, right? I'm not on a two year holiday. I have a job. I am an assistant language teacher (ALT) at Kotoh Junior High School, a ten-year old school with 550-odd students and around forty staff members.

In the next two columns, I'm going to tell you all about it. Gasp! at the whacky student hijinks. Shudder! at the plight of hapless English teachers. Smile! at the curious policies of the Japanese education system.

Yes, it's gonna be a wild ride. So, without further ado, I present to you, "A Day in the Life of Kotoh Chugakko."

8:13 a.m. – I arrive at school. I'm always one of the last teachers to pull into the parking lot. Upon entering the staff room, it's good form to announce "Ohayo Gozaimasu" ("Good Morning") in a voice that carries to at least the first few desks.

A quiet moment in the staff room. E. Sparling.

8:15 a.m. – The morning meeting begins. All of the teachers, including the Principal, Vice-Principal and Head Teacher, have desks in the staff room. When the bell sounds, we stand. The teacher assigned to lead the morning meeting (it changes daily) says "Ohayo Gozaimasu." We repeat the refrain. Then the Head Teacher announces the day's date. This is followed by people taking turns saying things in Japanese. I sit at my desk, oblivious to the critical announcements wafting through the air, and muddle my way through a Japanese correspondence course.

8:30 to 8:50 a.m. – More of me sitting at my desk, filling my coffee cup and attempting to master Japanese grammar. A few teachers remain in the staff room. Homeroom teachers go to their class rooms to start the day, while other teachers go outside to pick up wayward pieces of litter with long metal tongs. I've never been asked to help and I've never volunteered.

9:00 a.m. – First period begins. Periods are usually fifty minutes long, with ten minutes between them. There are four periods before lunch, each starting on the hour. But school schedules in Japan vary far more than schedules in Canada. Sometimes periods are only forty-five minutes. Other days, some grades will have classes cancelled; or there are assemblies, special events and rehearsals of all kinds. People often forget to inform the one non-Japanese teacher of the changes. Every assistant language teacher has had the experience of looking up from reading a book at their desk to see an empty room, with no clue where everybody went.

1:00 p.m. to 2:00 p.m. – Lunch time. Schools provide lunch for elementary and junior high school students in Japan. They eat in their homerooms. The kids retrieve big aluminum and plastic tubs of food from a truck delivery bay, and lug it to their classrooms. Once there, a few students don white kerchiefs and aprons, and ladle the servings out into bowls and metal trays. At the same time, classmates arrange the individual student desks into islands of friends.

Most of the staff eats "school lunch" in a small dining room. It's usually good. My favorites include miso vegetable soup and salmon with lemon. One bizarre feature of school lunch is that the smell in the halls when it's delivered is never an indicator of how it will taste. A nasty smell could still be a delicious meal.

Lunch is followed by recess. Then it's "soji" time. Cleaning.

Much is made of the fact that Japanese students clean their own schools. It's supposed to shape them into disciplined youngsters with respect for school property. Maybe it does. But while many students work hard during cleaning time, just as many do next to nothing. Some schools have novel ways of getting around this glut of lounging laborers. At one Matsue school, half of the students clean while the other half jogs around the grounds. They switch it up weekly.

2:10 p.m. – Afternoon classes begin with fifth period, followed by sixth. An interesting feature of Japanese schools is that the pupils stay in their classrooms for most subjects. It's the teachers who travel from room to room.

4:00 p.m. – The end of sixth period. The day is not over, though. The kids still have another homeroom meeting. Homeroom teachers play a large role in a student's life. Students write daily diaries which are reviewed by their homeroom teacher. The teacher may accompany a pupil who needs to see the school nurse. This teacher will also advise their charges about which high schools they should attend. A good homeroom teacher has a close rapport with his or her students.

4:30ish – Club training. Most junior high school students participate in school clubs every day: Basketball, kendo, tennis, brass band and more. This is a big time commitment. During the winter months, practice only lasts for a half hour or so. But when the days lengthen, so do the practices. Up to two hours is common in the spring and summer. And club practices are held on Saturdays, sometimes Sundays, and during most school holidays.

TEN

My mother lives in Peterborough. She reads the column, of course. This past Sunday, I received an email from her complimenting me on the latest installment of "Japan Diary." She did have one concern, however:

"It gave the impression that all you do at school is sit in the staff room all day."

Well, Mom, sometimes that's the case.

I have spent entire days sitting at my desk. I've tried to use the time constructively. I read long novels. I study Japanese a bit.

The government of Japan provides ALTs (my title) with the option of doing a Japanese language correspondence course. I have to pass five mail-in tests to get my certificate of "Beginner Japanese." I've passed four so far. Anyone wanna start a betting pool?

Yes, there are days, even weeks, when I do virtually nothing to earn my paycheck. Most days, though, I spend from one to five periods in the classroom helping a new generation of Japanese learn English.

The JET program—the program that recruited me to come to Japan—has been around for less than two decades. Prior to that, many Japanese children, and adults for that matter, had few opportunities to interact with foreigners. This was particularly true in less urbanized areas. They studied English in school but had very possibly never heard it spoken by a native speaker, except on tapes or in movies. The JET program was designed to rectify that.

The teaching method is called "team teaching." A native English speaker—me—is paired with a JTE, a Japanese teacher of English. We teach the class together.

The teaching experience varies depending upon the class, the day of the week or what flu is making the rounds that season. For the most part, it's fun. I try to make jokes in Japanese. The kids laugh—with me, at me, who cares?

My second year students are my favorite. I know, favorites are bad form for teachers. I can't help it. They're irreverent and funny. They can be boisterous, but give them a task and they're as goal-oriented as a cheetah chasing a Chihuahua.

The pace of grammar and vocabulary acquisition is break-neck. Many of these kids don't know the Roman alphabet at the start of junior high school. Most of them will be able to read simple passages, ask basic questions and express rudimentary opinions when they leave for high school. Their grammar might be poor and their confidence communicating verbally low, but they have a foundation.

Translation is out of favor among some language teachers back home. Personally, I learn best by translation. I have to admit, though, that there's probably too much of it in Japanese classrooms. The kids should understand new words through charades and spoken examples before they are told its Japanese equivalent. That doesn't always happen. Likewise, any story in the textbooks will inevitably be translated word for word.

Repetition is also a pillar of the teaching method. Many people with my job complain of being nothing more than "human tape recorders." If I had a hundred yen for every time I've announced to a class, "Now repeat after me...," I'd have something…um…really awesome.

There is also a troubling lack of emphasis on pronunciation. Many JTEs have poor accents. No surprise, so do their students. There are many reasons for this. The high school entrance exams don't have a verbal component, so it's not emphasized in the junior high curriculum. Many of the sounds in English don't exist in Japanese. Also, many English teachers have little overseas experience. They've never spoken English with someone who a) wasn't attuned to understanding the Japanese accent, and b) didn't slow down their speed of delivery and make easy vocabulary choices.

The JTEs are given a difficult task. They have to teach a lot of vocabulary and grammar in three short years. For the most part, they succeed. Many teachers and administrators seem to be aware of the system's shortcomings as well, and are taking steps, albeit slowly, to make changes.

Japan's acquisition of English lags behind other East Asian countries. Even so, the students at my school have better English than I have French.

The Japanese student: Sometimes portrayed in the west as a drone in an army of uniform—and uniformed—brainiacs.

This is, of course, not the case. Japanese students are sports stars and geeks, cool kids and bad boys, glamour girls and weirdos. Even their uniforms are not so uniform, what with small embellishments like ragged, low-slung pants for boys, oversized, slouchy white socks for girls and the degree to which a student's regulation plastic slippers have been mangled or graffiti-bedecked.

Some traits, though, are common. The students hate being singled out, even more than their Canadian counterparts. Group work is very popular. Stickers are a hot item as bribes for getting kids to volunteer answers. They're almost certain to genkify an ungenki class ("genki" is Japanese for keen or healthy).

The students are generally well-behaved, although two aberrations deserve mention. One is the incessant talking during classes—shameless, full volume conversation that, depending on which student we're talking about, barely diminishes when a teacher objects.

The second is, ahem, sexual. Japanese students are curious, to say the least. I get a laugh out of the two third-year boys who persistently ask me if I "like make love?" I'm not fazed when cheeky students ask my "size" (I just say, "ookii to nagai." I don't think I'll translate that for you.). I'm not quite as keen, however, on the third-year lad who insists on making a grab for my holiest of holys when he passes me in the hall. Many ALTs have had similar experiences. How do you say, "Back the #*%& off, son!" in Japanese?

ELEVEN

Our teenaged nephew has one request for a souvenir from Japan: A ninja throwing star. Although we've kept an eye out for one—they're called shuriken in Japanese—we haven't had much luck so far. It's a bit like asking a person who travels to France to bring back a matchlock dueling pistol.

I shouldn't tease him, though. The only thing many North Americans know about Japan is its martial past. That's fair. I'm gonna let you in on a little secret: Less than two years ago, I was one of those people.

Job interviews are fundamentally dishonest, aren't they? At my interview in Toronto for my current teaching job, I waxed on about my interest in Japanese history, geography and culture. The truth was, I knew virtually nothing about Japan or teaching English. I wanted to live overseas, I wanted to make money while I did it, and I'd heard good things about the Japanese Exchange and Teaching (JET) program in particular.

That was it. If a job with the pay and benefits of JET had been offered by the Myanmar Republic, we might be in Rangoon right now.

I did have one connection with Japan, though, and that was martial arts.

I tried my hand at karate many years ago. A few lessons, that's all. No offense—please don't chop me—but it didn't grab me. Wrestling, on the other hand, grabbed, threw and pretzled me. I wrestled at university for a year (badly, I might add) and that led me into judo, the Japanese art of grappling.

I did judo off and on over the course of two years, and while I never got good at it or completely absorbed in perfecting my technique, the joy of trying to choke another person kept me coming back for weekly workouts on a somewhat consistent basis.

So at least I had judo in my past. I thought that might be a trump card going into the interview. The one thing I was uncertain about revealing, however, was the only thing in Japan I had a strong desire to see: A Japanese castle.

Nothing to be embarrassed about, I suppose, except that my interest dated back to vague, childhood memories of the "Shogun" mini-series. I remember one scene where a guy commits seppuku, stabbing himself in the belly with a dagger. Some other dude got an arrow in the throat. Everybody looked really serious all the time and the Samurai warriors' mouths barely budged when they spoke. There were even ninjas creeping around, looking for someone to kill with my nephew's beloved shuriken.

Grisly melodrama, and all of it, in my mind, framed in the soaring architecture of Japanese castles.

Yes, the only strong impression I had of Japan was created by a made-for-TV movie.

I don't remember if I mentioned my "Shogun" interest in my interview, but I used it in

Kendo gear in a school's dojo. E. Sparling.

the essay that accompanied my application in the first place.

It might have even worked in my favor. Now that I've been here a while, my guess is that few Japanese have strong objections to the romanticizing of their warrior past.

I'm very lucky. The city we live in has its own castle, right downtown. It's even an original (most are reproductions). Our second day in Matsue, we went up to the castle grounds. It was so hot I thought I might die, but I still loved it. To this day it's my favorite place in the city. We also make a point of visiting castles whenever we travel to other prefectures. I refuse to say which is the best—I've loved every one I've seen.

As for martial arts, after a knee injury this past summer, I've moved from participant to spectator. We went to a sumo tournament in Osaka last year and the Judo World Championships this past fall. I regularly rent "Pride" videos—Japan's version of the Ultimate Fighting Championship—and I've even taken a few practice swings with a bamboo kendo sword. No stay in Japan would be complete without witnessing the spectacle of a kendo player in full regalia.

After we found out we'd been hired and we were going to Japan, I decided to read James Clavell's novel "Shogun." I loved every page of it.

I'll keep looking for my nephew's souvenir. To tide him over, we sent him a pocket knife for Christmas. It probably doesn't throw well, but I'm guessing it will have more modern applications than its feudal predecessor, the ninja star.

TWELVE

We had our first significant snowfall a couple of weeks ago. On that day, I got chatting with a friend, Kotoh-sensei, in the staff room at school. Kotoh-sensei and I usually speak English together, but on this occasion he took the opportunity to teach me a new Japanese word: Yukimizake.

Roughly translated, it means "Looking at snow falling while drinking liquor."

I like that. It should have been invented by a Canadian, but I like it.

It's hard to overstate the significance alcohol plays in Japanese society. It's not just a social lubricant. It's a social engine. And nowhere is this more evident than at an "enkai."

An enkai is a work party ("kai" rhymes with "guy"). School teachers have a lot of enkais, probably ten or more each year.

These parties usually kick-off at a hotel. Given that each person is paying anywhere from forty bucks to more than a hundred, these events are a huge part of a hotel's business.

Although the venues range from traditional to modern in décor, and the menus from simple (finger foods) to elaborate (six courses), the parties all follow the same trajectory.

Everyone makes an effort to arrive on time. Punctuality is very big in Japan. It's usually assigned seating, often with groups of four or five seated around large, circular tables.

Once the troops have gathered, it's time for a toast. Wait-staff zip around the tables cracking open the oversized bottles of beer that have been placed on each table. Colleagues then pour the beer into small glasses for each other. It's very bad form to pour for yourself. Once everyone has a glass, a senior member of the staff will shout "Kanpai!" which means "Cheers!" Everyone shouts "Kanpai!" in response. Then the eating and drinking begins.

The principal of the school might get just as hammered as the twenty-four-year-old P.E. teacher. The glasses are kept full. Have a few sips, and in a couple of minutes someone will be offering to top you up. If you want to chat with someone seated at another table, you pick up a large bottle of beer from your table, wander over and fill up their glass. Beer is the staple beverage, but nihon-shu is a popular second. Nihon-shu, also called sake, is rice wine. It's served warm or cold. I prefer it warm.

The first part of the enkai—referred to as the "first party"—only lasts a couple of hours. That's enough time for people to cut loose, though. Women are usually somewhat restrained. Male behavior, however, ranges from restrained to, well, not so restrained. An example? Gangs of young men in business suits will grab their supervisors and toss them in the air—birthday bumps minus the birthday. At another enkai I attended, the drunkest staff members were kneeling on the floor, bowing to people making speeches. (Think Wayne and Garth in the movie Wayne's World: "We're not worthy, we're not worthy!")

The first party typically closes with three shouts of "Banzai!" I'm still not sure what that means. Then everybody joins hands for a rousing rendition of the corporate or school song.

Most enkais will progress to a second party and sometimes on to a third, fourth or even fifth. Each "party" really just means a new venue: Drink at a place for awhile and then proceed to the next joint. Along the way, people drop out and go home.

A popular spot for these successive parties is a snack.

No, not a bag of chips and a soda.

A snack is a small bar. Matsue's drinking district—a warren of narrow lanes called Isemiya—is filled with snacks.

These places may be tiny, but the service is attentive and most of them still find room for a karaoke system. The hostess tops your drink up constantly and you can sing your Carpenters' faves until you're hoarse. Snacks aren't known for their drink selection, though. Don't bother asking for a Mai-Tai. Whiskey (usually with water), beer or shots of hard liquor are pretty much it.

This kind of rarified experience isn't cheap. By the time you divvy up the bill—always split evenly among participants—a visit to even an inexpensive snack might come to thirty bucks an hour for each reveler.

To try and sum up Japanese drinking culture in one column is impossible. It's not just enkais and snacks. It's also pubs and dance bars, nomihodai (all-you-can-drink establishments) and beer vending machines. And, of course, yukimizake.

Winter will be over soon. I never did get a chance to drink alcohol while watching the snow fall. I'm not too choked up about it, however. Come spring, there will be another drinking opportunity: "Hanamizake," otherwise known as "Looking at cherry blossoms while drinking liquor."

Beer vending machines. E. Sparling.

THIRTEEN

I am convinced that one of the main reasons tourists don't come to Japan is the language. It's intimidating. Without language, "Where is the bathroom?" becomes a humiliating game of charades.

Japanese doesn't use the Roman alphabet. It's not a European language, so to English speakers it probably seems more impenetrable than, say, Spanish or even German. And despite the large number of Canadians who have worked in Japan, it's still extremely rare to see anyone speaking Japanese in Canada who isn't themselves Japanese or Japanese-Canadian.

So, in the interests of parting the mists of incomprehension, I would like to provide you with a short description of Japanese.

No, I'm not trying to pull a fast one here. My feeble language skills are well-documented. But in the land of the illiterate, the man who can read the "Men's washroom" sign is king. I might lead you astray, but not as astray as you'd be just opening your mouth and making random sounds.

Japanese, like most languages, is a mix of domestic and foreign words. In the past, Chinese was a huge contributor to Japanese. This is evident in the use of *kanji*—Chinese characters—in the written language. More recently, English has invaded Japan, albeit in an altered form. More on that later.

Japanese uses three kinds of characters: hiragana, katakana and kanji. The first two consist of 46 characters each, but there are thousands of kanji characters. In addition to the 46 basic characters, hiragana and katakana symbols can be altered with the addition of small marks or even mini-versions of themselves.

The end result is that it takes a heck of a long time just to know enough symbols to read simple sentences.

The good news about the written language is that, once you know the symbols, Japanese is easy to pronounce. Hiragana and katakana were created so that each symbol represents one sound and one sound only. In English, you don't know the pronunciation of a new word until a native speaker demonstrates it for you. In Japanese, you can just read the string of symbols, with equal emphasis on each sound, and you usually won't go too far astray.

The Japanese have a tough time pronouncing English. This is because some English sounds simply don't exist in Japanese, for example "see" or "th." This is also the source of the notorious difficulty Japanese people have with "r" and "l." They have a sound that lies right in between the sounds of these two consonants. The same problem confronts them distinguishing between "v" and "b."

English may be difficult to pronounce but my hosts have a solution. They just speak English with a Japanese accent.

Tons of English words are now part of the local vocabulary. Take "convenience store" for instance. Here it's shortened to "kon-bi-ni." The word "cake" becomes "kee-ki" and "television" becomes "te-re-bi." There are hundreds, perhaps thousands of these words. To distinguish them from native words, they are written in katakana. That is the sole function of katakana: to let the locals know that the word they are reading is an import.

On the plus side, whenever you don't know the word for something, you can just say the English word with a Japanese accent, and you'll often luck upon a katakana word.

Well, there you have it: Japanese in a nutshell. This, combined with my handy vocabulary list, should have you ready for Japan. Oh, you'll still be utterly confused, frequently lost and unable to understand virtually anything that's said to you. But the Japanese people like English-speaking foreigners and the crime rate is low. Someone will help you eventually. If all else fails, you can stand in the middle of a shopping mall and shout, "Ta-su-ke-te!" That means "Help me!" Someone will come on the double just to shut you up.

You didn't think I'd just abandon you with a couple of quips about toilets, did you? Language consists of words, and words you shall have.
Subjects:
I = wa-ta-shi
you = a-na-ta
this = ko-re
Verbs:
play/do = shi-ma-su
go = i-ki-ma-su
come = ki-ma-su
want = ho-shi-i de-su
have = mot-te i-ma-su

Nouns:
food = ta-be-mo-no
drinks = no-mi-mo-no
taxi = ta-ku-shi
money = o-ka-ne
hotel = ho-te-ru
Essentials:
How much does it cost? = I-ku-ra de-su ka.
Please speak English. = E-i-go de o-ne-ga-i-shi-ma-su.
Where is the bathroom? = To-i-re wa do-ko de-su ka.
I don't understand. = Wa-ka-ri-ma-sen.
Pleasantries:
please =ku-da-sa-i
thank you = a-ri-ga-to
hello = kon-ni-chi-wa
bye-bye = bye-bye

In basic English sentences, the order is subject-verb-object: "I play basketball." In Japanese, it's subject-object-verb: "I basketball play." (In Japanese: "Wa-ta-shi wa ba-su-ke-to o shi-ma-su.") If you're writing Japanese with the Roman alphabet, you use "a, i, u, e, o" for the vowel sounds. These are pronounced "ah, ee, oo, eh, oh."

FOURTEEN

Sometimes living abroad becomes tiresome. The exotic things become mundane while the inconveniences of a foreign language and culture remain. I'm not complaining, just stating a fact. One of the best ways to remedy this has to be getting out of your own little neighborhood and seeing more of your host country. Tanya and I decided to do just that for our eight-day spring vacation.

Kyushu is the most southerly of Japan's four main islands. With a tent and sleeping bags purchased via the Internet from Canada, we resolved to jump in our car and head down to Kyushu for some sightseeing.

For our first stop on the island, we decided to go to Nagasaki. While the journey to Nagasaki from Matsue can be made in one day, it's more pleasant broken into two half-days of driving. That was our plan.

We left Matsue on a Saturday morning with a full load. We have a fourteen-year old Mitsubishi "k" car called a Dangan (Japanese for bullet). The Japanese "k" denotes a car with an engine of 600 cc or less. Think motorcycles.

Into this gallant little warrior of a car, we stuffed ourselves, our tent, packs and sleeping bags, plus another ALT, Percy, who wanted a lift to Nagasaki.

Our first overnight was still on the island of Honshu, at a campsite near the entrance to Akiyoshi-do, a vast cave.

You could play a game of football in Akiyoshi-do. A concrete path wends its way down a long tube of soaring roofs, deep cliffs, bizarre rock formations, pools and a river, eventually emerging in a tastefully manicured, wooded glade.

We visited the cave first thing in the morning and were on the road to Nagasaki well before noon.

The islands of Honshu (where we live) and Kyushu (our destination) are separated by a thin channel spanned by a bridge. Despite their proximity, the tourist literature assured us that the two islands were quite distinct in character. Residents of Kyushu were portrayed as friendlier than people from Honshu. Percy told us that the stereotype of men from Kyushu is that they are macho.

Kyushu is famous as the foreign gateway to Japan. Most of the nation's Chinese and Korean influences came via Kyushu. The island is close to the Korean peninsula. The Mongolians twice tried to invade Japan through Kyushu. On both occasions, the Mongolian fleets were destroyed by storms. The Japanese named the nation-saving storms "kamikaze," which means "divine wind"— the name later chosen for the Japanese air force's suicide missions in World War II.*

Nagasaki is known abroad for being the second city struck by the atomic bomb. It is equally famous within Japan, however, as an "open port" during the Shogunate era, which stretched from the start of the 17th century to the end of the 1860s. To

Akiyoshi-do. T. Sparling.

minimize Western influences, the samurai restricted European trade to Nagasaki.

Upon exiting the highway and proceeding into Nagasaki, we were immediately struck by one difference between it and other Japanese cities: The number of buildings and homes built on the hillsides. In general, towns in Japan are built on plains, valleys or river deltas. Nagasaki's neighborhoods and streets cascaded down the surrounding slopes.

We dropped Percy downtown and immediately headed north to our campground. We were reserving the city itself for later.

Our camp ground was up in the mountains of the Nagasaki Prefectural Forest Park. The drive up to the site was beautiful albeit a bit hair-raising. The roads were narrow and windy and, really, how much faith can you have in fourteen-year old brakes?

We spent Monday, the day after our arrival in the Nagasaki area, at our camp ground. We hiked a short trail into the woods, crossing a pedestrian bridge over a gorge—man, I hate heights—and finding a shy lizard holed up in an earthen embankment. Tanya spent ten minutes trying to get a picture of the little fella, but the two times he poked his head out, it coincided with her brushing hair out of her eyes. We continued on our way before frustration could give way to lizard assault.

We were in bed early that night in preparation for a good start to a day in downtown Nagasaki.

We awoke to pouring rain. Not a big deal, except that we were moving to a new campground, south of Nagasaki, at the end of the day. Taking down the tent in the rain was a chilly task.

Cherry blossom season in Nagasaki. T. Sparling.

One day is not a lot of time to see a city. We had three priorities: see the atomic bomb museum, visit the garden built on the site of the old European quarter, and get a piece of cake.

We had already been to the Hiroshima Peace Park and museum. While both are important to see, I found Nagasaki's museum more affecting. The first few chambers of the Hiroshima museum devote a lot of space to the history of the city and a reckoning of global nuclear stockpiles. The Nagasaki museum, in contrast, plunges you almost immediately into the events of August 9, 1945. It's illustrated with gruesome photos that are horrific and absorbing at the same time. All of the facts of that day are provided in grim detail before moving onto the larger dilemma of nuclear proliferation.

We emerged from the museum to dwindling rain and a renewed hope that we might get to see the city without getting completely soaked.

Our next stop was the entertainment district. We were on a mission to find the home of Fukusaya, the oldest purveyors of Castella, a Japanese cake based on a Portugese recipe. They have been making Castella by hand since 1624, although the shop location where we bought our cake was only a couple of hundred years old, give or take a few decades. The confection itself was like a richly-flavored, dense vanilla sponge cake. I tucked into the loaf like Homer packin' down a passel of Pop-Tarts.

A walk uphill took us in the direction of the old European quarter. The European quarter itself is long gone. It's been remade, after a fashion. The Glover Garden, named for a prominent Scot who lived in Nagasaki at the turn of the last century, has pleasant paths and a number of period homes that have been removed from their original locations and rebuilt in the garden. We started at the top and made our way down the hillside, taking in the great views of the harbor and moving quickly through houses kitted out in "exotic" Western furniture familiar to any Canadian antique lover back home.

It had turned into a gorgeous, sunny day. With weary feet we headed back to our car, then drove south to the Shimabara peninsula and our next camp site.

* *Background information for chapters fourteen and fifteen from the* Lonely Planet Japan *guidebook.*

FIFTEEN

Tanya and I took advantage of our recent spring break to head south to the island of Kyushu. As I mentioned in the last column, after seeing a massive cavern en route, we passed a couple of very pleasant nights camping in a mountaintop forest north of Nagasaki. We then headed down to Nagasaki for a day of exploration before continuing south to our next camping location in the Shimabara peninsula.

The drive from Nagasaki to the peninsula follows the coastline of a broad bay. We passed by small farms with green crops and sandy beaches. Looking out to sea, in the haze on the horizon, you could make out the outline of mountainous islands. Palm trees dotted the side of the road.

All of these features were lovely, but most impressive of all was the approaching peninsula. Shimabara-hanto (hanto means peninsula) is composed of two large volcanoes. The summits of the peaks were obscured in cloud, but the forest-covered slopes were spectacular in the yellow light of the closing afternoon.

Our camp site was halfway up the other side of one of the mountains, so our drive took us right up the slope and then partway down again. The following morning, we drove back up one of the volcanoes to the spa town of Unzen.

People travel to Unzen to bathe in its natural hot springs. Walkways are built over ground that bubbles with boiling water and sulfurous gases. We wandered around the village for a couple of hours. The closest I came to a bath was eating some eggs that were hardboiled in one of them. The highlight of our visit, though, was a stop at a pottery shop.

The proprietors were a husband and wife team who had converted part of their home into a studio. Their work was magnificent and justifiably expensive. The entrance room, however, had a selection of attractively earthy, modestly priced work. We selected a uniquely shaped sake bottle. When the proprietress went away to pack it up for us, we got talking and decided to get a couple of cups to go with it. She then insisted on giving us the two cups as gifts.

It's surprising how often we are the recipients of this kind of kindness. There's really no polite way to refuse, even in a situation where North Americans might consider a gift inappropriate, for example when a journalist is interviewing someone—for example, a potter—and the subject of the story gives the journalist a present. (Tanya assures me that my professional objectivity hasn't been tainted forever.)

We left the peninsula the following day by car ferry, crossing a massive bay to Kumamoto.

Kumamoto prefecture is located on the western side of central Kyushu. It is home to Aso-san, the world's largest caldera volcano. According to www.dictionary.com, a caldera is "a large crater formed by volcanic explosion or by collapse of a volcanic cone." Aso-san has a circumference of 80 kilometers.

The giant, natural amphitheater is sequestered from the rest of the world by a ring of short, steep mountains. In the center of this vast bowl are five volcano cones, remnants from the enormous volcano that formed the original caldera. The peaks are in excess of a thousand meters tall.

This exotic setting is home to a number of small towns and villages, green farms, horse trekking ranches and the closest thing I've found to Japanese hippies.

As we drove along a road, looking for the turnoff to our camp ground, we came across a cluster of businesses and restaurants.

There was a gift store, with bamboo rain-makers, hemp trinkets, cans of vegan chili and CDs of animals grunting—all granola cruncher stuff that I occasionally enjoyed back home, but in Japan was like an oasis of New Age consumerism.

There was a bakery that had muffins, a broad selection of breads and even two kinds of quiche, none of which are a sure thing in Japanese bakeries.

There was a little pizza joint, constructed out of a red trailer and decorated with vintage Coke knick-knacks. The guy behind the counter had slicked-back hair and there was Dad's Root Beer in the fridge.

The pick of the litter, though, was the Kachina Trading Western Shop. Constructed to look like a building out of the movie *Tombstone*, it was stuffed to the gills with more cowboy memorabilia than you'd find in the states of Texas, New Mexico and Arizona combined.

Framed replicas of sheriff's badges. Incredibly tooled saddles. Hats and boots. Lamps, shirts, mugs, jewelry—you name it, they had it. The

Path to the crater's edge. T. Sparling.

couple who ran the place spoke great English. They also had a dog named Bonham, after the legendary Led Zeppelin drummer who drank himself to death.

I'd never looked into a volcano before. They're not exactly plentiful back in Canada. So, the next day, we drove up yet another winding, dangerous road to the summit of one of the five cones.

Access to the rim of the crater was by no means a sure thing. If the scientists stationed there determine that the crater is volatile, you aren't allowed up to the edge.

That was the case when we first arrived. Great, billowing clouds of white steam and gases rose into the sky. Another crater, inactive for the moment, was accessible. It looked like an open rock quarry, with smooth clay at the bottom. We wandered around, taking in the lunar landscape of black, volcanic sand and multi-hued rock strata. Just as we were about to give up, they removed the barrier and allowed us to walk right up to the edge of the active crater.

You couldn't make out much, really. I wanted lava, rivers of the stuff, but all you could see was steam.

Lava or no lava, the whole spectacle of Aso-san was impressive. We left with a newfound respect for the diversity of Japan's landscapes.

On our way back to Matsue we overnighted near the city of Hagi. Hagi is known for two things: one of the city's sons played a role in the Meiji Restoration in the mid-1800s, a revolution which wrested power from the feudal samurai class and invested it in a bureaucracy that was devoted to modernization. It's also known for Hagi-yaki, a pottery style that's ranked among the best in Japan.

We passed an enjoyable afternoon wandering through Hagi's old samurai quarter and admiring Hagi-yaki before retiring to our camp ground.

As is usually the case when I travel, I arrived back in Matsue the next day pleased with the new things I'd seen but also content to see the journey come to an end. The following week, the last school term of our stay in Japan began.

SIXTEEN

I read in the Globe and Mail newspaper a short while ago that when federal politicians want to take the pulse of Canadian voters, they poll Peterborough. Apparently, you represent the mainstream of the nation.

I don't know how residents of Peterborough feel about being designated "the middle." I suppose moderation can be a good thing, if a little staid.

Inherent in talking about the mainstream is generalization. You talk in broad sweeps, neglecting sometimes significant anomalies. At the risk of painting a stereotype, however, I would like to take this opportunity to tell you, Canada's supposed middle, what constitutes Japan's mainstream views on a broad number of social issues.

If you're pressed for time and want to skip the rest, let me give you the short version: Sometimes the Japanese make Pat Buchanan look progressive.

Tanya and I have an acquaintance that was born in Japan. Her parents were born in Japan. Her grandparents, however, were not. They were born in Korea. Hence, she is a Korean and is required to carry an Alien Registration Card, just like Tanya and me. She even has a Korean passport, although she's never been to the country of her so-called origin. In fairness, she would probably be a good candidate for acquiring Japanese citizenship, what with her Japanese family (husband and kids) and good job (she's a neurologist). To do so, however, would require an involved application process.

While some Canadians wrestle with the newly legislated legality of gay marriage, many Japanese wrestle with showing gay people basic civility. I was invited to a social studies class at my school to talk about Canada. The teacher is interested in internationalization. He's lived abroad and pushes his students to think beyond their prefecture. However, when I was asked to talk about Toronto's biggest festivals, my description of the Pride Parade elicited a bizarre reaction. The teacher drooped his wrist and started prancing on the spot like, well, a fairy—you know, the woodland spirit creatures. Other assistant language teachers (foreigners, like me) have reported Japanese people who won't even acknowledge that our prefecture "has" gay people.

I would be grossly remiss if I didn't mention the status of women. The examples of inequality could fill volumes, never mind a newspaper column. Just one: At a recent PTA meeting, the member-parents in attendance were overwhelmingly women, while the PTA board (seated on chairs, as opposed to the floor, like the women) consisted of one woman and perhaps ten men.

In Japan, a woman's place is definitely in the home. Of course, there are working women, lots of them. But many are working only until they become mothers, and even if they then continue to work, they are grossly overburdened with domestic duties at home. Friends have expressed surprise that I often make my own meals. After all, that's

Tanya's job. Even at work, it falls to the women to fetch tea and snacks for distinguished visitors.

North Americans have a contradictory attitude towards animals. We see some as pets and others as food and the reasoning that separates the two is fuzzy at best.

I'm not going to get shrill about this. Yes, Tanya and I are animal lovers (Tanya's a vegetarian), but reasonable, compassionate people can disagree about the moral status of animals. There are good people who hunt and animal rights activists who are jerks.

In Japan, however, I don't think it's occurred to most people that the issue of morality and animals needs to be considered at all.

In Kochi prefecture, they stage dog fights. Tourists arrive by the busload. When we visited Kochi, I was initially interested in seeing a bout. The fights were billed as "demonstrations," which sounded fairly innocuous. Just to be safe, though, we decided to skip it. I was glad we did, because one of Tanya's colleagues later confirmed that the matches can get bloody.

At an aquarium we visited, they had a cement fishing pond in the center of the facility. Yes, the kiddies could marvel at all of the beautiful exhibits and then catch a fish of their very own to munch on.

Our local department store, Saty, has ivory for sale. Japan is one of 166 "parties" (nations) that have agreed to be bound by the Convention on International Trade in Endangered Species of Wild Fauna and Flora (CITES). And yet, a 2002 press release posted on CITES's website says that Japan is one of the countries where elephant products are "openly traded." According to TRAFFIC, an organization with close ties to the UN-administered CITES: "These markets are generally poorly regulated and, to a large extent, rely upon illegal sources of ivory for the production of curios."

The owners of a campground we stopped at in Kyushu had a medium-sized turtle in a small aquarium on their front counter. The aquarium was literally a glass box—no water, no vegetation, nothing. In Canada, I'm pretty sure a customer would tell the owners to get their act together.

The restrictions the community imposes on individuals in this country would be funny if they weren't so stifling. A friend of mine from Chicago was threatened with having his teaching job terminated because of the type of helmet he wore when he drove his three-wheeled scooter. It's black and has a red, feathered crest running along the top, like a Roman centurion's head gear. Silly? Sure. Unsafe? Definitely. But the law here doesn't even require him to wear a helmet. He could drive his vehicle bare-headed.

Regardless, our Board of Education (BOE) thought it was scandalous. He was ordered not to wear it, even outside of work hours. If he insisted on wearing it, he would be fired. (Update: The BOE has talked about softening its position but Cleve still hasn't been told that he can wear his helmet.)

It would be easy to dismiss all of this as the product of a rural backwater. Shimane is a conservative part of the country. But given that Tokyo's governor is a notorious nationalist, it's hard to be optimistic about more enlightened attitudes prevailing in metropolitan centers.

These negative observations don't trump all of the positive comments I've made in previous columns. For the most part, the Japanese are generous, polite and kind. There is simply a massive awareness gap in this nation when it comes to social issues or alternative viewpoints.

Tanya must be bored of hearing me say it: Japan is the way I picture America was in the 1950s. Ironically, this view was basically confirmed by our supervisor at the Board of Education.

"Japan is three decades behind North America," he said.

He didn't seem too concerned about it, however. The Japanese people "are flexible," he said, they will change when they need to.

Well, they need to. In the year 2004, being thirty years behind the curve is a crisis. Rapid change needs to happen now.

SEVENTEEN

The Japanese approach to recreation is, in a word, crazy.

They tackle their fun the way they tackle their work—with dogged determination that often borders more on duty than delight.

I don't recall when this fact was first brought home to me. It may have been in the first few weeks at my school, when I was thinking about getting involved in the extra-curricular lives of my students. You know, maybe hang around after school a day or two a week, playing sports or some such with the kids.

I decided to do kendo and table tennis—one session of each, each week. This seemed like a maintainable, positive commitment to getting to know my students and having some fun doing it.

With that simple act, I immediately set myself apart from my colleagues and young charges.

"Doing clubs" in Japan doesn't mean a sane, hour-long piano lesson once a week, or a Saturday morning soccer practice. No, clubs in this country are a time commitment on-par with a part-time job: Practices every day after school, weekends and almost every holiday, including summer vacation. It's a tiring schedule, especially when most of my students report that they aren't getting to bed before eleven and many are up until one in the morning or later.

At the end of last summer, I was perusing through student diaries (assigned by their English teacher). More than a few had diary entries that read: "I am very tired. I had clubs yesterday. It was very hard. But I will fight!"

The end result is a uniformly high-level of weary skill. The chronic over-training almost certainly impedes the attainment of true excellence. (To quote an Irish colleague: "For the amount of training they do, Japan should win every medal at the Olympics. But they don't!")

At least this insane pace eases when the Japanese enter adulthood. Of course, it's replaced with long hours at work. These long work hours leave little time for recreation. What recreation there is seems to divide along gender lines, with a couple of tawdry exceptions.

The men drink. At an enkai a few weeks ago, a colleague was insistent that I should come out to the "second party," the next drinking establishment on the itinerary for the evening. I told him I couldn't, that my "wife was waiting for me." His response? "My wife is waiting for me, too, but I'm going!" I informed him that the difference between us was that I actually wanted to go home. Another friend informed me—with a rueful smile, at least—that he was very tired because he was out drinking all night and woke up in a strange girl's apartment. Good thing his wife was at home to care for their young daughter and toddler son.

This behavior is by no means unique to Japan. What was bizarre, however, was that, at the time, I didn't know this man that well, yet he felt his behavior was commonplace enough to share with me.

The women generally engage in more civilized behavior: Having four dollar cups of coffee with friends, going to the movies, learning a musical instrument, or studying traditional art forms, such as the tea ceremony, calligraphy or making pottery (although all of these activities have male participants as well). Women can't devote the same amount of time to their hobbies as their children do to club training or their husbands to drinking. Mothers and wives are responsible for all of the household domestic duties while often holding down a full-time job as well.

There are two forms of recreation, however, in which the both genders take part: pachinko and infidelity.

Pachinko parlors dot the urban landscape with their neon lights and sometimes bizarre English billboards. I've never played pachinko. I'm not a big fan of gambling. I gather that pachinko is like a cross between pinball and slot machines. You win metal balls which you then trade in for goods. It's illegal to win cash. The goods are traded for cash at a pawn shop, which is often conveniently located right outside the pachinko parlor.

As for infidelity, I've heard that it's widespread. I don't have percentages on it. Who am I, StatsJapan? I do recall reading somewhere that the genders are equally likely to stray. There is a place for everything in Japan, including extra-marital trysts. They're called love hotels. The rooms are rented by the hour and some have themes—astronauts and aliens having close encounters of the carnal kind, perhaps.

Intent on throwing a pot. T. Sparling.

The final feature of Japan's leisure life that bears mentioning is modesty. Complaining about a tough workout is fine, but that's as close as the Japanese come to bragging. People typically understate their skill.

If a Japanese person says she's "good" at music, it probably means she's First Violin for the Tokyo Philharmonic Orchestra.

EIGHTEEN

What are the three best views in Canada?

Every Canadian would have his or her own answer to that question. Niagara Falls might appear on a lot of people's lists. Maybe Lake Louise. I don't know my final three but Peggy's Cove would be a contender.

In Japan, there is an official answer to this question, dictated by age-old tradition. Japan's three best views are: a bay on the island of Miyajima, close to Hiroshima; a stretch of scenic coastline north of Tokyo called Matsushima; and Amanohashidate.

We decided to use our Golden Week holiday—an annual event in Japan—to drive east along the Sea of Japan coast to Amanohashidate. You've already been introduced to some of this rural coastline's highlights—the pottery town of Hagi, the castle city of Matsue and the sand dunes of Tottori.

We left Matsue on a Friday morning. Our tent was stuffed in the back of the car, along with study materials for the MCAT (Tanya) and GameBoy Advance (me). We arrived in the little village of Hotaino in the late afternoon. We would have made it more quickly but we took a couple of wrong turns. We missed the turn-off for the final road into the campground, an absurdly narrow track between two houses that hardly warranted the designation "driveway."

We stretched our legs that evening by walking into the village. It was lovely: rice paddies, bamboo-covered hillsides, large farmhouses and small trucks, old women in bonnets and old men in green work pants.

Hotaino is located inland from the Tango-hanto, a bulge of land that extends into the Sea of Japan. The next day, we took advantage of the fine weather to explore the area.

Our first stop was a bay twenty minutes north of our campsite. Only a narrows connects it to the sea. A bridge closes the gap.

I was almost immediately impressed. It reminded us a little of home. Perhaps it was the Jet-skis zipping across the flat water or the appearance of some of the restaurants. I knew they wouldn't have a clubhouse with fries on the menu but they looked like they might. The roads had that strange mix of development and countryside that is common in Ontario's cottage country or out in Nova Scotia, Tanya's home province.

In the afternoon we decided to follow the coast road of the Tango-hanto to Amanohashidate.

It was spectacular. The road dives up and down mountains, with steep, rocky slopes dropping away into the surf. As the afternoon grew late, we stopped in the fishing port of Ine. The distinctive shoreline homes have boathouses incorporated into their first floor. After checking out the main street, we took in the view from the sea on a half hour boat tour.

Unfortunately, though, we were running out of time. Our last stop of the day, Amanohashidate, was the whole reason we were on the trip. A scenic view in the dark isn't very scenic.

My fears were not entirely unjustified. As per usual, we missed our stop and had to backtrack. We finally found the right place with only fifteen minutes to spare.

"But Eric, what the heck is Amanohashidate?" you ask. Well, it's a thin finger of land that crosses the mouth of a bay, creating a salt water lagoon. The "bridge" doesn't quite reach the south side, leaving a narrow channel, but from an elevated vantage point it looks like it touches.

We arrived in time to take the second last train to the top of a mountainside overlooking the bridge. It's more an elevator, really, a single car pulled by a cable that climbs the slope at a steep angle.

The view itself was quite pretty but I don't know if its lofty reputation is deserved. It's an interesting coincidence that all three of the "best views" are located on Honshu. I wonder whether Japan's other three islands got equal consideration.

There is even a sanctioned way to take in the view: Upside down, peering between your legs. Apparently the idea is that the bridge looks like it's floating in the sky, hence the name Amanohashidate, which means "bridge to Heaven." I just found it disorienting.

Sunday morning we decided to spend the day a little closer to our camp-site. We drove north again, in the direction of the coast, to the onsen town of Kinosaki.

An onsen is a natural hot spring. The Japanese are crazy about them. They take entire

The bridge to Heaven. T. Sparling.

holidays which consist of walking around a spa town in a robe, stopping at different spas to have a bath. The thrill is lost on me.

Kinosaki was not without appeal, however. Despite the choking traffic, the small town was quite pretty. A narrow river spanned by pedestrian bridges runs through the heart of the spa district. Mingled amongst the tourists are people dressed in yukatas—summer robes—and wooden sandals making a pilgrimage to their next bath. I decided to drop into one of the public baths for a quick cleanse. I emerged half an hour later, slightly refreshed but still mystified by the reverence my hosts have for this national pastime.

With a couple of hours left in the day, we drove 10 kilometers north to Marine World, an aquarium built on a picturesque stretch of rocky seaside. The aquarium was a mix of interesting and depressing. I love to see animals but hate to see them in boxes.

When we arrived back at our campground that Sunday evening, it had started to fill up a bit. On the first night, we'd had the whole place to ourselves. Golden Week is a popular time for domestic travel and Hotaino is a day's drive from Osaka and Kyoto. Although we'd had a wonderful couple of days, the weather forecast was predicting rain the next day. We expected more campers, too. We decided to cut our trip short by a day and head back to Matsue the following morning.

My spirits were high but the drive was tiresome. At times the traffic was bumper-to-bumper as people headed out for the holidays. At one point, going through a tunnel, we were passed by a big black bus, its windows covered with protective metal fencing. The Japanese flag was painted on its side and militaristic marching music was blaring deafeningly from mounted loud speakers. No doubt the local contingent of some nationalist party.

This year the Golden Week holiday consisted of three days, Monday through Wednesday, plus the previous Thursday. With Saturday and Sunday coming before Monday, that made five days in a row. In Canada, the Monday would be a good day to drive—right smack in the middle of the holiday. But not in Japan. I don't know if people had to work on Saturday and Sunday or what but it seemed like every car in the country was on the roads Monday. Then, when we finally got back to Matsue, it was comparatively quiet.

Holidays in bathtubs, fascists on field trips, five-day weekends cut needlessly down to three and one of the country's finest views turned upside down. Sometimes, the longer I live in Japan, the stranger it seems.

NINETEEN

You find the prettiest places right in your own backyard.

The Oki islands are part of Shimane prefecture (where Matsue, our home, is located). They are divided into two parts: Dozen and Dogo. Dogo is the largest island. Dozen is a group of three islands in the shape of a horseshoe.

When Tanya and I first applied to teach in Japan, I was excited to find out we were coming to Matsue but a little jealous of the handful of people who were posted to Oki. Its remoteness seemed exotic.

My jealousy of the Oki teachers faded over our first year. One Oki person quit. Most of the others put in for a transfer. At least they had the option. Historically, people who fell out of favor with Japan's ruling elite were banished to Oki.

My interest in seeing Oki never faded, however. With our departure from Japan looming this summer, Tanya and I took the opportunity to visit for a long weekend.

Rather, it was supposed to be a long weekend. We even arranged to have the Friday off from work. But then Tanya's supervisor at school, Makino-sensei, suggested joining us. He'd worked on Oki his first year as a teacher, perhaps two decades ago. A Japanese teacher never takes a

Friday off from work. Our long weekend became a regular weekend.

We left for Oki on the Saturday morning. The weather was overcast. I hoped the seas would be raging. The crossing is notoriously unpleasant in winter but surging swells sounded exciting to me.

No such luck. As we passed our first hour, almost halfway, the seas became bigger but not big enough to make my stomach churn.

The first glimpse of the islands was quite dramatic. Our destination was the Dozen group (pronounced "dough-zen"), in particular Nishinoshima, the largest of the three and home to about 4,000 people. The steep, black shapes emerged out of the haze in the distance. The three islands form a vast, deep lagoon. Originally, they were part of one large volcanic cone.

We stopped first at the island of Chibu, the smallest of the three, before continuing on to our destination. The rocky cliffs and verdant green hillsides looked wild and empty in the gray light.

Our ferry docked at Nishinoshima. We emerged to the sight of Oki islanders dancing on the wharf. Some sort of welcoming committee. There were maybe ten of them, middle-aged. They wore happi—a bright blue, kimono-style shirt worn for festivals.

Another person was there to welcome us: Oketani, Makino's friend. After an unremarkable lunch (I had seafood spaghetti with ketchupy sauce), Oketani escorted us to his small van to begin our tour.

People come to Nishinoshima for three things: the scenery, the horses and fishing. I'm not much of a fisherman. That left scenery and horses.

The road into the mountains was steep and narrow but there was virtually no traffic. I say virtually because as we climbed higher we began to run into cows. Not literally, of course, but we'd come around a bend and there would be a cow or three in the middle of the road.

We emerged onto a ridgeline. The view was phenomenal in every direction. In one direction, however, was the postcard, the scene that appears on the tourist brochures. A series of cliffs rise up from a cove, the tallest 257 meters above the water. Minarets of igneous rock rise out of the sea. And in the center, there's a huge stone arch.

After driving down to the cove for a closer look at the arch, we drove back-roads up to the pinnacle of the cliff we had already seen from afar. When we stepped out of the van, the wind was intense. The peaks around us were partially obscured in fog and clouds gusted across our path.

Cows aren't the only animals that roam loose on Nishinoshima's hills. There are also horses. A small herd grazed in the pasture between the parking lot and the cliff. There was even a colt. I admire the beauty of horses (despite the jokes I make about turning my cousin's pony into hot dogs). Tanya was in heaven, however. She had pet horses growing up. She would have been content to sit in the pasture for hours.

The height afforded us a panoramic view of the surrounding coastline.

I steeled myself to look over the cliff's edge. The waves looked very, very small below.

As we headed down the mountain, I asked our guide about the horses: "Does someone own them?"

A classic Oki view. T. Sparling.

Yes, he responded, farmers. The farmers sell the horses to butchers in Kyushu.

That kind of sucked some of the romance out of the "wild horses" of Oki.

After a brief stop at a three-room museum—some interesting artifacts, but small museums in a foreign language aren't great—we arrived in Oketani's hometown. Makino-sensei was staying with Oketani's family. They had made arrangements for Tanya and me to stay at a hotel. It was only three or so in the afternoon but our guides were already jettisoning us. We knew there wouldn't be much for us to do on an overcast evening in a tiny fishing village. I didn't expect to get screeched-in or anything, but some socializing with Oketani's family would have been nice.

We also weren't entirely pleased when Makino announced that, if the weather was nasty (as forecasted) he wanted to head back to Matsue first thing the following morning. Our long weekend in Oki had become a day and a night.

All was not lost, however. As it turned out, the hotel we were staying in was a ryokan—a traditional Japanese inn. It was a first for us, so I was excited about finally having the experience.

Ryokan accommodations are old school: straw mat floors (called tatami), thin "futon" mattresses to sleep on (placed directly on the floor), Japanese-style bathing facilities and sliding doors (usually a wooden latticework covered in paper). Some include meals in the price.

A ryokan was a welcome change from the cramped and sterile business hotels in which we usually stayed.

After a walk to a gray-sand beach and a bento meal (literally "box lunch"), we returned to

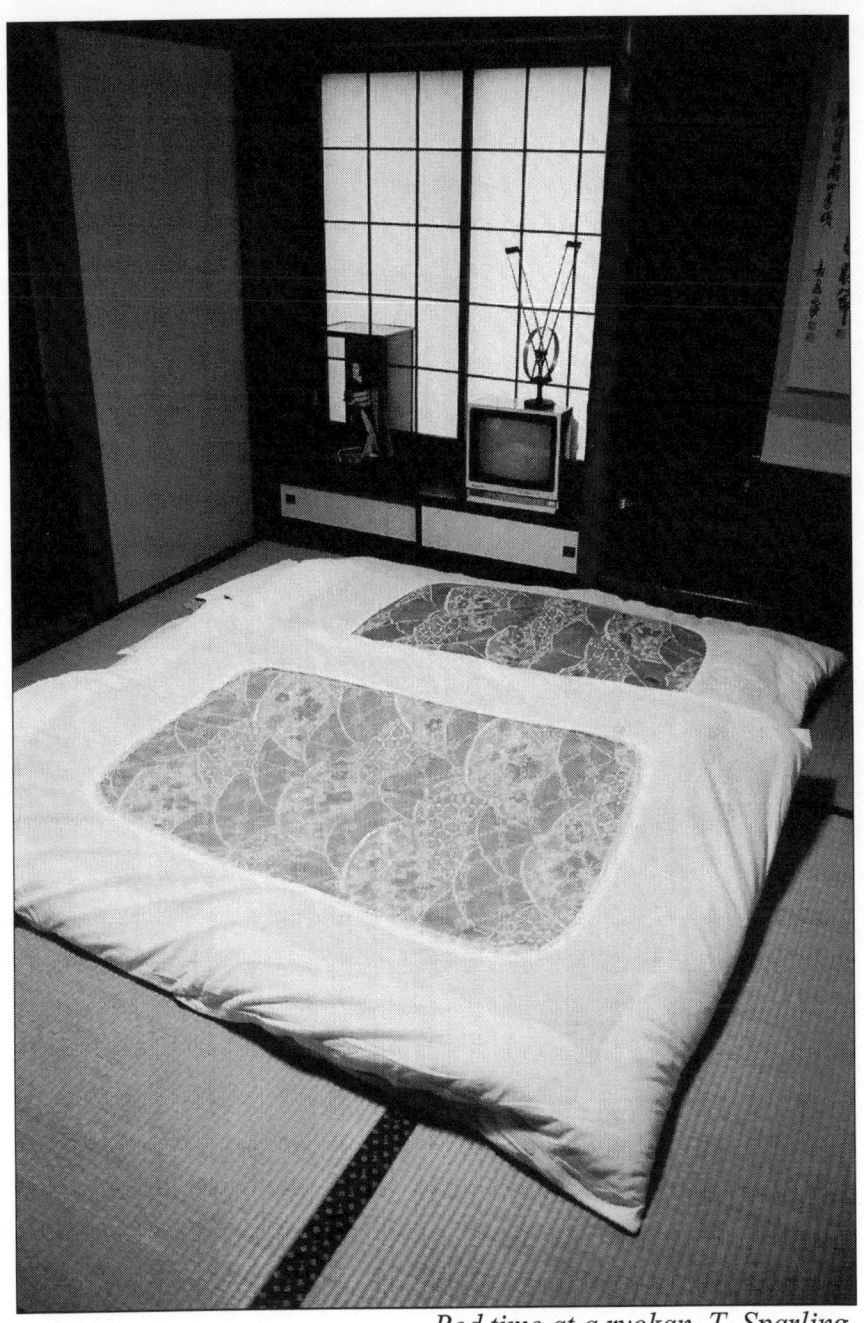
Bed time at a ryokan. T. Sparling.

the hotel for a bath. The Japanese bathe at night. If you're staying at a ryokan, you do the same. When we returned to our room, the low table had been moved and our futons had been set out. We turned in for the night soon after the sun set.

We weren't surprised to wake to a gray morning and the patter of rain on the tile roof. Despite the disappointment of knowing we were going home early, it was pleasant in the cool, dim room, listening to the rain come down.

On the trip back across the sea to Honshu, I remarked to my traveling companions that the ideal living-in-Japan experience might span three years and three places: a year each in Hiroshima, Matsue and Oki—large, medium and small. I wouldn't want to be banished to Oki for life but if I ever wanted to spend a year in Japan cultivating a love for fishing, Nishinoshima would be a great option.

TWENTY

Tanya and I were in Japan only a few weeks when we went to Hiroshima for the first time. I remember being excited about our premier trip in-country. There was also the sense that we were going to see something important.

Hiroshima isn't just a city. In the minds of people around the world, the name evokes one image: Atomic devastation.

On August 6th, 1945, at 8:15 a.m., the Enola Gay dropped Little Boy on the city of Hiroshima. Five hundred meters from the ground, the bomb exploded, almost instantly killing tens of thousands.

On that first visit, we saw the A-Bomb Dome, we walked through the Peace Park and we toured the large museum at the park's center.

It was a grimly fascinating experience but, of course, it was impossible to feel the full magnitude of that distant day's horror. The scene of so much carnage is now a beautiful green space. The rivers that frame the Peace Park, choked with bodies some 60 years before, are a perfect spot to take a photo of a loved one.

On that weekend, almost two years ago, we discovered more than just Hiroshima the Bombed. We discovered Hiroshima the Beautiful.

Tanya and I are returning to Canada at the beginning of August. Although I saw Hiroshima for a second time with a buddy last fall, Tanya hadn't had a chance to go back. With fond memories of our previous overnight visit together, it seemed only fitting that we should book-end our stay in Japan with a return trip to Hiroshima.

We took a bus down on a Friday afternoon. The city, backed by mountains, is located on a broad delta on the coast of the Inland Sea. We were deposited at the Hiroshima bus station, conveniently located in Sogo, a massive department store just minutes from the Peace Park, the shopping district and our hotel.

After checking in at our lodgings, we made a beeline for Kemby's, a western-style restaurant and drinking joint. For foreign residents of the comparatively isolated Matsue, a trip to a big city usually entails consuming vast quantities of North American food; in this case, a platter of nachos, vegetarian fajitas, and a cheese and tuna quesadilla (the memory of which I will always cherish). The night was rounded out with a stroll through the massive pedestrian arcade, absorbing the sights of the big city.

Our upbeat, vacation mood took a blow the following morning. Tanya discovered that her wallet was missing. She was pretty certain she left it in our hotel room the previous night. Japan has a very low theft rate. Still, it was hard to imagine a credible alternative. We were pretty sure we were robbed.

The weather wasn't cooperating, either. The rain the forecasters were predicting had moved in on the Friday night. It was supposed to continue throughout the weekend. This put a damper on the two pillars of our plans—a baseball game and a return trip to the picturesque island of Miyajima.

The Hiroshima Carp had home games that weekend. Although I'm not really a baseball fan, I thought it might be interesting to go.

Luckily for me, the rain slackened Saturday afternoon. I headed off to the stadium—like most of the city's noteworthy sites, right downtown—hoping to see bizarre and exotic baseball rituals of the East.

I was not disappointed. The game itself is universal—same rules, same viewing experience. What were different were the fans. Hiroshima's stadium is fairly small, much smaller than Toronto's Sky Dome. On this particular afternoon, it was less than a third full. I was in the cheap seats, by the outfield, the most densely populated part of the stands.

The cheering began at the same time as the game. I never knew such a small crowd could make so much noise. Some of the fans had trumpets, while others had drums. These were used in coordinated fashion. Everyone knew what to play and when. Accompanying these instruments were the bulk of the fans, chanting, waving their hands, and sitting and standing in unison. This fascinating, albeit exhausting, spectacle was coordinated by a cheerleader—in each section, one person, wearing a "Carp Club" jacket and white gloves, stood on a seat and led the assembled masses in their demonstrations.

One fan was waving a massive flag with a skull on it and "Sex.Gamble.Baseball" written across the top.

If you became exhausted from all your efforts, you could fortify yourself with popcorn or a steaming bowl of noodles. There was even a young guy in lime green running around with a small keg strapped to his back.

During the seventh inning, the fans performed another ritual: Releasing the rockets. Long, vaguely phallic balloons were inflated by the crowd and then released simultaneously. The hundreds of balloons whistled as they rose into the air.

The Carp had a good day against the Yokohama Bay Stars. A grand slam helped. The final score was 11 to 4.

The weather cooperated for the baseball game but not for going to scenic Miyajima. When we woke the following Sunday morning, the rain was steady. We decided to cut our losses and head back to Matsue that morning.

Honestly, we felt a little deflated. Our last big weekend in Japan was a bit of a bust. We were settled back into our apartment, girding ourselves for another week of work, when the phone rang. It was our supervisor from the board of education. He'd received a call from the bus company. They found Tanya's wallet, including more than $150. The seemingly impossible—that her wallet was stolen from our hotel room—was just that.

The weekend might not have measured up to our hopes but Japan's reputation for honesty certainly did.

Lying just west of Hiroshima is the island of Miyajima, ranked among Japan's three finest views.

It's a short ferry ride across from the mainland. The steep, tree-covered slopes of the island's mountains provide a perfect backdrop to

The famed torii of Miyajima. E. Sparling.

the cluster of red structures on the shoreline. Two structures are most prominent—a nearly thousand-year old shrine and a massive torii. Torii are wooden gates found at the entrance to shrines. The base of Miyajima's torii is submerged when the tide is in. The same is true for the shrine.

Elsewhere on the island is a warren of pleasant tourist shops, often quite full with bus tours and school trips. Semi-tame deer wander around, always ready to make a meal of anything that's left unattended.

The brave can take two successive cable cars up one of the mountains. The hearty can hike it. At the top, there are great views of the Inland Sea. There are also wild monkeys. Signs warn tourists that monkeys don't like to be stared at—they see it as a sign of aggression. Being soundly beaten by an enraged primate would have to be one of the more humiliating and painful experiences one could have in Japan.

TWENTY-ONE

I'm a big fan of ice cream. Mint Chocolate Chip, Hoofprints, Cherry Garcia. The day they invent healthy ice cream is the day I forswear all other forms of nutrition.

Or maybe not. As the saying goes, too much of a good thing isn't a good thing.

For example, I've never tried to down six liters of Rocky Road in one sitting. If I did, I think the experience would go something like this: Bite one, awesome. Bite forty-three, still awesome. Bite one hundred and ten, only good. Somewhere around bite two hundred and six, I'd stop having fun. Oh, I would still intellectually know that Rocky Road was delicious—and that sometime in the future I might want a five-scoop bowl of it—but on a visceral level, a gut level, I'd be done.

You're on to me, aren't you? That's right. I'm not really talking about ice cream anymore.

I've kind of struggled with this, the last entry in the Japan Diary. You see, I'm down to the last few spoonfuls of that six liter vat. I'm ready to come home.

I feel like a bit of a heretic saying that, like it might be seen as an admission of failure on my part. It might sound a little uncouth, like a slap in the face of an entire nation or a dismissal of two years of my life.

Well, it's none of those things.

Living in Japan has been an incredible experience but it doesn't fit neatly into the script.

You know that script. It's filled with uplifting platitudes about cultural understanding and the global village.

The truth is, there have been days when I have cursed this country and its residents. There have been days when the rich tapestry of Japanese culture has felt smothering; when I would have gladly traded a gorgeously executed tea ceremony for a cold Snapple and a surly convenience store clerk.

In the past two years, there have been magical moments as well; peak flashes of insight when I knew that what I was seeing—what I was feeling—was being indelibly printed in the part of my brain labeled "Important stuff."

My new school welcoming me with a stirring rendition of Canada's national anthem. Or the first time I heard Kimigayo, Japan's majestic and haunting anthem. Kicking off a shoe and placing my foot in the Sea of Japan. Seeing a suit of samurai armor, except that I wasn't in the Royal Ontario Museum, I was in Matsue castle. Looking out the window of a bullet train that keeps going faster and faster.

There's been no shortage of natural beauty: Kyushu's volcanoes and Shikoku's coastline; New Zealands's fjords and Borneo's nature preserves.

And, of course, small personal victories. I passed that Japanese correspondence course. I wrote a ridiculously long novel. The fact that it's bad only diminishes my pleasure in having written it by a little.

After almost six months of weekly pottery classes, I finally made one piece of which I'm truly proud.

I wrote a bi-weekly column for the Peterborough Examiner.

These last few months, however, the scale has started to tip a little. The positive flashes aren't as intense and the incidences of frustration have increased.

Does that mean that living in Japan was a mistake? Absolutely not. I'm just glad we didn't sign on for a third year.

I'm not off ice cream entirely but I'm gonna pass on the Rocky Road for awhile. These days, I have a mighty strong hankering for Maple Swirl.

One of the things I like best about traveling is that it increases my appreciation of home. I like Japan. I just like Canada better.

My heart will lift a little when we touch down at Pearson on August 5th.

Kansai airport. E. Sparling.

Made in the USA
Lexington, KY
27 January 2012